I0151836

RECLAIMING THE DEAD

RECLAIMING THE DEAD

Miriam N. Kotzin

NEW AMERICAN PRESS

Fort Collins, Colorado

NEW AMERICAN PRESS

© 2008 by Miriam N. Kotzin

All rights reserved. No part of this publication may be reproduced, stored in a retrieval system, or transmitted, in any form or by any means, electronic, mechanical, photocopying, recording, or otherwise, without the prior written permission of the copyright holder.

Printed in the United States of America

Distributed by Ingram Book Group and Baker & Taylor

ISBN 978-0-9817802-2-1

Grateful acknowledgment is made to the editors of the following publications, where many of the poems in this book first appeared:

BLAST, Blaze Quarterly Literary Magazine, Blowback, Boulevard, Branches, Confrontation, Drexel On-line Journal, Facets, Flashquake, Mad Poets Review, The MAG, Mid-American Review, nthposition, Open Wide, The Philomathean Society Anthology of Poetry in Honor of Daniel Hoffman, Plum Ruby Review, Poetry Super Highway, Press 1, Segue, Southern Humanities Review, Taurus, Three Candles, and *Word Riot.*

CONTENTS

Repose   11

Honeymoon   13

Astronomy Lesson   15

The House   17

Invocation   33

Separate Vacations   34

Dawn   37

Landscape   39

Wisteria   41

Divination   44

Spring   46

Daylily House   47

Awakening to Zinnias   48

Sunflower   50

Acapulco Holiday   52

Cliff Divers   54

Taxco   56

Coconut Death	59
The Pond	61
Woods Water Moving Picture Poem	64
Night Visit	65
Birds	66
Souvenirs	67
Two Ways to Get to the Same Place	68
Catechism	71
Middle Age	72
Aubade	73
Infestations	74
Shards	75
Ritual	77
Clairvoyant	79
Elegy for a Woman	80
Yardwork	82
The Copper Bowl	83
Portrait	87
Seafood	89

Assemblage: Altered Object   90

A Woman's Poem   92

Challenge   95

Seder   97

Checklist   99

Gravesite   100

Reclaiming the Dead   101

Housekeeping   103

Keeping Time   104

Harvest   105

Lois Lane Courts Death   107

Still Life   109

Dancers   112

Mystery Lovers   114

Lycanthropy   115

For my parents

Dr. Isadore Kotzin and Frances Scheiber Kotzin

R e p o s e

The little white blossoms
whose names I do not know
are in flower. The branches
bend with the weight
of their whiteness.
I'd learn their names
to say as I pass what is in bloom,
as today I say iris, rose,
rhododendron, peony, lilac,
holding them by their names
though I cannot stay the season.

A woman hanging clothes turns,
lifts her hands to the line,
bends to the basket,
lifts to the line, bends
like a weighted branch.
I watch with your eyes
aspects of gesture captured.

In me you found less gesture
than a certain stillness,
an arrangement of hair,
the curve of my arm above my head.

•

As you held me, I will hold
you in these words
while the tall iris withers,
and the rose, rhododendron, peony, lilac
and all the little nameless blossoms.

Honeymoon

The maples sweeten with the season;
the landscape in twilight is harmless.
Through drawn curtains I glimpse
hidden interiors, dimly lit.
I wonder whose lives, in passing,
I've flattened into a set.
This is the time to learn
to trust in darkness.

Unseasonably you mention peach blossoms
"White in the wind." We are far
from peach orchards. All country
is the same to you. Peach blossoms
are not white. They are pink.
To you orchards of blossoms
are nothing but poetry.
I've studied blossoms,
feared late hard frosts,
waited to climb for the highest fruit,
known sun, the crick in the neck picking,
known the weight of fruit.
"Petals like snow."
I say nothing. Instead

•

I lean towards you
as I lean into the wind,
drawn off balance,
seeking new equilibrium.

Astronomy Lesson

Like the ceiling of an old
motion picture palace,
out here, moonless, the sky

is perfectly tacky with stars.
As I walk towards you,
skymaps become pointless.

So all the mythy figures move
across the sky with the slow
pageantry of half-remembered legends

or remote projections
in a planetarium. These
specks of light do not illuminate

the fields below or the mice in the corn
stubble cowering as the owl swoops, then
feathering the night with little cries.

Nonetheless, you are standing
immobile in the pale yellow oblong
of the lighted window, a steady

•

solid darkness towards whose form
my own slow motion is directed.
But really the stars are burning.

The House

1. The Hall

Here the house pivots.
We can go in any direction
in this clutter of entrances and exits.

The chandelier needs washing;
the carpet treads are grayed.
The house has gotten away from us.
We know so little of one another now
as though I have wakened from a long sleep
to find you changed by a journey.

Yet this octagonal hall seems
a geometer's dream of elegance:
the hexagonal rug, its pastel pattern
knotted by distant fingers,
the inlaid Chinese chests,
the gilded mirrors,
the old photographs of families.

I watch the changeless moons
of their faces.
Slowly the hall fills
with pale light,
the lost beauty of women.

2. The Dining Room

Suddenly you noticed the walls
in this room
where we two
were so seldom alone together.
How many nights
you sat at the head of the table
like some prideful pasha,
the room gleaming with crystal and silver,
bright with linens and china,
while I shuttled like some useful undersecretary
eager to serve.

How lucky we were
to be surrounded by so many
who knew a melon spoon when they saw one.
On Sunday they followed the hounds;
on Monday through Friday they followed the Market,
but we all followed
the good, the true and the beautiful
from consommé to demitasse and brandy.
Oh, I am being unfair and peevish;
these people meant us no harm.

You found the walls here drab, undistinguished.
Deciding what to match,
rugs, drapes, chairs,

you've been preoccupied for weeks
leering at sample books of papers.

Now we are alone together in this room,
and I hold up lengths of wallpaper
like a hopeful draper's assistant.
The blue and white is too insistent.
We soon will tire of these bowing mandarins,
frozen in their formal postures.
The gold floral is too lavish,
a B-film vision of a New Orleans bordello.
I do not look my best dripping in rhinestones
in a red-silk dressing gown,
sporting white ostrich plumes in my hair.

The patterns we have tried will not do.
The walls will have to stay as they are for a time
while we return to the search
determined to find the right touch.

3. The Living Room

In this ice-blue room
nothing of consequence ever happens.
The Roman glass in the case
is iridescent as soap bubbles.
You've placed the Chinese pieces

to best advantage.
You are an authority
on dynasties and glazes.

One summer evening
the women left the men
for the dusk
as generations of men
have left us for cigars.

It was the time between two suns
crickets   birds falling silent   crickets.
Twenty-five years ago
we would all have been giddy
with such an evening.
But we were silent
as we walked across the long lawn
down to the stream
and the willows rising dark
against the darkening sky.

We counted three stars
the new moon.
Yesterday we prayed for life, peace, joy
deliverance and consolation.
The Big Dipper, the Little Dipper.
While we watch,
the constellations multiply.

Tonight none of us
needs the North Star.
White dresses.
Our skirts flutter
in the darkness.

We walk back up to the house
through French doors
into a world furnished with Chinese Chippendale.

While we sit
moths gather on the screen
pressed flat to the light.

4. The Den

Wall to wall real
color-coordinated
overstuffed
another working fireplace
upholstered and three
antique painted decoys
with mail order
cleverly mixed in with
all this custom-made
coziness.

Night after night
we sit
side by side
in the flickering
light of
Spencer Tracy and
Katherine Hepburn and
Fred Astaire and Ginger
Rogers and Debbie Reynolds
and Donald O'Connor and
Rock Hudson and Doris Day
and the thought for the day
and old glory
until finally the room
falls silent
and we know
all the happy endings
are over.

5. The Kitchen

We meet here mornings.
On the table the lazy Susan
is a gaudy roulette of vitamins.
A tangle of plants
grows up around the fireplace.

Our first winter when it snowed weekend mornings
we had long breakfasts here,
the world in soft focus.
Then the land fell off into whiteness.

Suppers now are a World Affairs Council
seminar for two—broiled chicken, rice
and Great Ideas almondine.
I used to find your earnest references
to the Movement touching.
But there have been too many Movements,
too much change in our own lives
to be easy in these conversations.
I know your lines and mine,
but I'm not looking for surprises.

A flat of seedlings is on the counter
in the best light.
The pale green spindles bend to the sun
like a corps de ballet caught
in a graceful gesture.

In nice weather we ate on the terrace.
You've come to hate the smell of citronella,
and the mosquitoes have gotten worse.

•

From the kitchen we can see down to the trees,
the woods to the West,
the willows near the stream.
Often lately I've stood idle at the sink,
my hands still, looking out, watching,
half-expecting to see a phoenix
gold and red
rise up in flames from the greening willows.

6. The Basement

In descent we were always uncertain.
Perhaps the sense of a darkness
so suddenly disturbed unnerved us.

Here is the machinery that keeps us going:
the unexpected starts of motors;
the nearly silent hum of meters,
measuring, always measuring.
The sump pump and French drain:
when water finds its level,
the pump starts.
I am afraid of floods,
of accidental electrocutions.

•

It's a place of smells.
The crawlspace under the kitchen's dank.
I do not wish to shine a beam there,
to disturb unimaginable creatures,
to have them scuttle noisily away
from the light. Or rush towards it.

In spite of all our precautions--
dehumidifiers, drains, pumps--
the walls are efflorescing.
White flowers of crystals
crumble under the lightest brush
of our fingers.

Irresistibly we are drawn to this decay
everywhere invisible: in the pipes, slow
corrosion; through all the insulation,
inevitable losses.

7. The Guest Room

We inhabit the past
amidst this furniture
from thrift shops and attics.
These pieces, shabby in the city,
have become picturesque
in this country house:

the bureau, vanity, night table,
all covered with embroidered scarves;
the white hobnailed lamp,
not real milk glass,
but somehow right for this room.

The drawers and closets
are almost filled
with whatever's out of season,
our half cast-offs.

The prints that go nowhere else
are hung here.

The vanity, two sticky drawers
on each side of the center shelf.
How many women
have sat on this low bench
leaning towards their flawed image,
becoming in turn hair,
eyes, lips, never wholly themselves,
then lifted their arms
to twist their hair
into an easy order.

•

Whoever sleeps here
will wake to three beech trees,
weeping, copper, cut leaf—
shimmering in the sun.

8. The Study

Cordoned, this room's closed to me.
On each chair a printed card,
"Do not sit on this chair";
on the desk and shelves,
"Do not touch."

The lounge chair
with its own rug
is an island of itself
surrounded by scatter
of bright shoals,
magazines and books you've read
or mean to read.

The desk's a muddle,
yet I have watched you
unerringly reach.

•

The bookshelves are Dewey-decimaled.
No books lie on their sides,
as though you've been left
a meager passion,
a librarian's legacy.

Primitive paintings,
strangely joyless
landscapes and portraits
hang everywhere in this room.

9. The Spare Room

Furnished wholly by light,
as much as any field or forest
this room changes with the seasons.
White walls, bare oak floor,
uncurtained windows;
this room is always filled
with rising and falling intensities.

The light shifts,
brightens and dims,
is gold or gray.

•

I am often alone. Restless,
I move from room to room
until I find myself here.

Bright winter afternoons,
I bring in a thick khaki blanket
and lie like a cat
in the sun.

10. The Master Bath

Whose dream was this?
Mirrored tile, white marble, gold swan spigots.
The swans extend their necks,
mouths open in a silent squawk;
their wings lift.
To this room we've added an old chair
enameled white.

Tonight after a bath
I see myself pinkly fragmented.
My body folds into itself;
the white towel falls:
tendrils of my hair escape
the swift knot.

•

The clerestory window's
open to the sky.
A three-quarter moon
hangs in the corner
haloed by mist.
I switch off the light
and move among the shadows.
The moon splinters on the tiles.
I am a ghost figure
moving in silence
among the glinting swans
poised for flight.

11. The Master Bedroom

We wanted to anchor ourselves here.
The furniture's dark, heavy.
The four-poster bed,
covered with ivory lace,
an ivory canopy.
We chose these rose walls,
painted the woodwork ivory.

Over the mantle
a landscape:
a simple rhythm of trees
in unchanging bloom.

When I became your wife
we stood under a canopy
wound with flowers.
With seven blessings
I circled you seven times.
You crushed a glass
beneath your heel,
O Jerusalem.

Our friends, dancing,
lifted us on chairs
high above their shoulders.
Past our first youth,
yet we were buoyant;
we had no thought of falling.
We held a handkerchief
pulled tight between us.

Grace.
Seven blessings for our marriage.
The blessing for wine.

I used to come to you
each month, husband,
as a bride again
to her bridegroom.
Now, back to back

we lie apart
as though we choose
to keep our distance
while we sleep.

Still I dream in this house of rooms.
I dream of a breaking glass.
I dream of seven blessings.
I dream of circling you still
in this house of rooms,
circling endlessly as the moon.

Invocation

Wanting to wake you, I try your
name, softly. Your nickname does not
whisper well. I whisper all your
names: the liquids and sibilants, the
vowels fill my mouth; my tongue lifts
to my palate, it touches my teeth,
and my lips press your name. When
I whisper your name, sleeper, your
name escapes me, and yet when I
breathe, my breath whispers you.
Perhaps

        if I were to go to the sea, my
mouth stuffed with syllables, whispering
into the wind, the waves wild, the water
still wine-dark, Venus would return,
scudding to shore like a surfer,
and take pity on me. And you, sleeper,
you would hear and wake.

Separate Vacations

Sleeping, you travel
without me to places
we have never been.
You hug your pillow,
burrow, ignore the tug
of morning light.

Our room is strewn
with your unpacked bags,
left where you dropped
them from your sleep.
Or have you traveled
light, one flash-blue bag slung
over a shoulder? I stumble,
tripping into your sleep.

Some nights I travel, too,
clamber, nimble as a goat,
up hills where the white
stone in August noon
is dangerous as snow.
"Sunblind," whispers a woman
in black beneath an ancient
tree whose silver green leaves
cast blue shadows on the
terraced hillside. She will

34

not look at me, but I know
she is the old woman in
the snapshot where
you clutch her skirt and
hide your face in long
dark folds of cloth.

Or I travel to water,
find a garret room
with a narrow bed
by a wall with two windows
overlooking the sea.
Or I find my way
to the old hotel
on the far shore
of the lake of dark water.
There, on a wide porch
silent men and women
sit on rocking chairs.

The chairs creak.
An ant makes its way
across the concrete floor.
The woman who leans
against the pillar
near the stairs
could be your sister.

•

Sometimes, travelers
waking, we come so
close to one another,
we almost touch.

D a w n

If I want to sleep, still
night; it could be
morning. I want to
peer into your dream-
raddled sleep. "O,"
my mouth round,
I want to enter your
dream, to be your air, be
your light glinting on
water, be light
on the white rocks
of your safe shore.
"O," my mouth open as
an egg, I cipher my-
self, but I want to hear
your sleep-muddled
voice speak my name
as you wake. "O," I
enter the air, reach
you turning, hear you
murmur, "Mmmm."
I glimpse water, solid
with light, white
rocks. Then you wake on
a dime. Small change if
we're to bodies

gone. "What is it? Is any-
thing wrong?" "O," I
say, "O," the kindest
truth I can think of, "O,
Nothing, nothing."

L a n d s c a p e

Hills are not exactly anything
after the melt, snow patched like
mange on backs of slow
beasts. Now, gray and brown,
in changing light the hills shift
their weight.

           In softened air
we watch the line of distant
trees for blush. Like tourists
off the Gloucester coast,
scanning for the tell-tale
spout that hangs, shimmers,
fades, we wait to call
the sighting; the huge back
breaks the surface, rises,
and in a splendid curve
descends; or perhaps the fluke
stands, held, as in a crude
woodcut in a book of yarns
we can take from the shelf,
and after a puff of dust
is blown from the top edge,
open whenever we choose.

•

From stubble and matted grasses
a few tufts rise; hopeful plumes
move in light wind.

Wisteria

1.

I am a rainwoman mourning
in a world of water.

The windows are glazed with water.
The lawn slopes away from the house
down to the stream where willows grow.
Yesterday after the storm
you went down at dusk
to gather willow branches
torn from the trees by the wind.
You came to me,
your arms filled
with dripping lashes.

We are unable to translate
the wisteria heavy with rain.
We will not go walking
through fields of high wet grasses
to return home drenched.
You recede like an indifferent figure
seen from a train.

•

This morning I am a rainwoman
in a house of water
where I am lost
to a receding indifferent figure.

2.

I am a rainwoman dancing
among the willows.

Bending, swaying,
my body brushes
the streaming branches.
My dance trails
a wake of motion.

The land falls away from the house
as I have fallen slowly away from you.

The drooping wisteria
no longer pose their riddle.
I have unlocked their mystery
with my dance.

•

In the watery light of morning
the willows tremble
with their memories of a rainwoman
dancing,
body swaying on banks
of a boundary stream.

Divination

I polish the small brass
bowl. When I show it to you,
you look down into it, smiling
at your reflection. So, for
the first time in a long while,
I hold your face in my hands.

While you are away at work,
I melt fine wax in the bowl.
I pour the wax slowly onto cold water.
I watch two figures in the film:
their limbs entwine. Later,

I find an excuse to take your hand.
The Mount of the Moon, of Venus,
of the Sun, of Saturn, of Jupiter.
I see what I know. I do not confuse
the pale traces of scars with
character. The line of love goes
straight across: You seek intellectual
companionship, you are fastidious
and passionate. Tomorrow

I will build a fire to study
the flames. I will cast three
stones on the still surface
of the pond. I will brew tea.
I will serve chicken
for dinner. I will see what
I know. I will not confuse
scars with character. I
will hold your face
in my hands. You will smile
at your reflection in my eyes.
We will learn what we know.

Spring

I watched the full-bloomed magnolias,
pink and white, spill
into a pool on the lawn
until one day I woke
to see you stand
under the tree,
slightly stooped,
your back turned to the house,
and with swift movements rake.

At last the wisteria
is blossoming uncontrollably.
Someday I will follow the stream
away into the woods
where the water widens
to a seeming stillness.
There watercress grows wild
in the cool, slow current.

Daylily House

The house is surrounded
by lilies we fry for supper.
We eat the body of summer.

The mist rises.
Over the hayfield
the mountains reappear.

The light in the woods
is green as water.
We wade through ferns.

The bushes are heavy
with berries. Our fingers
stain red with the picking.

Beaks deep in delphinium,
hummingbirds slake
a ruby-throated thirst.

Awakening to Zinnias

Awakening, I see only scarlet
breaking open my sleep
carefully, like separating an egg,
detaching yolk from white.
Each petal becomes clear,
flowering until my world is one
great flat world of petals, a flower-
head with a dark red eye, star circled.
I see only scarlet, then sleep breaks, opens
just beyond scarlet to magenta, cerise, to
kiln-fired pot: orange, sienna, white, to
leaves, paired, lanceolate; the pot
marked by heat, darkened.
Now I see nothing but scarlet,
orange, yellow, cream, magenta, cerise
petals in circle after bright circle
quickening. All I see, waking,
roused from my sleep on the
sofa, is color, then petals, zinnias,
the kiln-flred pot, all these
undulating. The thick stems, sinuous;
veined undersides of petals.

Waking, I find myself
x-ing out everything inessential.
Yes, I say to scarlet, magenta, orange, to
zinnias, until the whole loose
arrangement becomes clear, and then,
across the room, you.

Sunflower

The leathery leaves droop:
the stem, fibrous as straw,
dries; the bright halo,
gone. Still the heart
of the sunflower is shot with light,
surprising glints in the black
center, as an old mirror
brokenly reflects, in worn
silvering, droplets of incidental
light, as my dark center
catches careless sparks,
keeps them.

I leaned on the ledge,
attempting the casual.
When you'd gone, I looked
at my palms; in the noon
sun my hands
glittered with mica,
held light
unexpected as the sparkle
at the heart of the sunflower,
dark and furred
like the pelt of an animal
hidden at night in the
desert whose cries

inhabit our dreams,
reminders of unwelcome
desire.

I rip away petals,
look into the mirror
of the flower, look
into my own eyes,
reflections giving back
my image smaller,
fruitlessly multiplying,
returning myself to my-
self until I disappear.
Unless, perhaps, you, too,
have some recollection
of a field, the heads
of the flowers too heavy
with seed to follow the sun.

Acapulco Holiday

Each evening the sunset
offers itself up like
a gaudy sacrifice
we've come to expect, but
it plays itself out as
grudging, insincere. We

watch the gold flare to yet
one more brilliance; a spike
of crimson repeats twice:
the trailing clouds are cut.
Another evening has
given way to night. Three

days gone. Four. We forget
why we came here. We strike
up talk with strangers, price
blankets, bargain for what
we do not want. The jazz
band plays New York sounds. We

grow careless, the regret
we once felt is gone like
lost small change. Local ice
laces drinks: coconut
filled with rum razzmatazz;
still no mariachi.

Cliff Divers

They perch on the sun-washed cliff or
in dives timed to the rush of water
soar, poised mid-air in our photographs.

Like a cheap tropical prop, one large
palm tree holds the wind still.
Time is marked by a disorderly

gathering of boats in the currents
of a sea far too blue. I am caught
off guard by his absence, and then

I recognize him standing behind the girl
in the yellow dress, his white shirt
pulled taut over his back, his arms

folded over his chest, a characteristic
pose. I am mistaken. I chide myself
for failing to put him at the center

of the scene, until I remember how
he left me in the crowd to buy cold beer
for both of us and returned to stand

•

behind me, his hand on my shoulder
while we watched the divers, even then
knowing they were less reckless than we.

T a x c o

Santa Prisca is hung
with plastic for restoration.
We sit in cool darkness, listen
to stories of old promises
of salvation and gratitude:
"I will give you my child.
Lord, I will give you my child."
As we leave the church
we hear trumpets. Women and
small girls arrive, wearing
black dresses, carrying white
carnations. We step aside.
Behind them, pall bearers,
black coffin, weary musicians.

In every store, heavy silver
necklaces, bracelets,
brooches, rings, tea services,
goblets, money clips. Wearied
by so much gleaming,
we merely glance at the tables.
We stand together on a balcony
for someone to take a picture of
us smiling at the lens,
behind us an indistinguishable
green. We could step backward

into air, over the gloating town
built on treasure. When I find
a small dish of inexpensive rings,
delicate thin turnings of silver,
I show them to him.
"What are these for?" he asks,
as though I held out a tray of fire
opals and diamonds. High in a palm
tree, a black bird whistles.

I stand after luncheon,
looking out over the valley.
We had eaten familiar foods.
Onions, slivered, opened
to chrysanthemums.
Tomatoes, peeled,
twirled into roses.
He has shaped
my heart into a
strange tropical flower.
With a few more deft motions
he turns my heart
into a bird in flight.

Last night yellow lilies
shot across my sleep
like stars, hollow shells
I crack open to read my future.

Now when I think of him,
he disappears behind a screen,
scarlet as cascading bougainvillea.

Coconut Death

It sits on a shelf,
stares into the room
with dumb face
that for us is filled
with fresh intelligence.

Once, impassioned,
we would have rained blows
until it split,
spilt the viscous liquid
center everywhere.

Now we go by the book.
We've read
The Joy of Cooking.
We know how to use heat
to crack the shell,
how to tap briskly
to make it come
neatly apart, spilling
not one drop.

However it happens,
we pare away the rind
and shred the sweetish meat.

Ravenous as ever,
barely civilized,
we still share
the savage feast.

The Pond

Over the pond the tree swallow
stitches the evening. From below
the surface, eyes stare,
curious from where
danger is rare; yet although

the frogs are safe for the moment,
a large shadow is a portent
of menace. A blue
heron swoops; he's new
here. We view his descent

from the porch, the Adirondack
chairs, our easy seats, no drawback
to the drama. We
watch the shadowy
waters. We both lean back

after the strike: silver wriggling
fish held fast in the beak, a niggling
shame in our delight
in the struggle, bright
in twilight, silvering

death. No. Rather it is merely
transformed, fish to fowl, and, as we
watch, the fish takes flight,
scales feathered. Twilight
deepens. Night's colony

of silence is unsettled.
Imperfectly the world is held
night's thrall. The peepers
and bullfrogs—the leapers—
and creepers' voices swelled

so that the small flitting bat
seems caught in a lariat
of swift rising sound
and then spun around,
up and down, acrobat,

albeit unwilling. But wait.
The lariat stills. Quiet. The gate
swings open. No one
speaks. The evening is gone.
We are alone. It is late.

·

The moment has passed and the small
ghost of desire gone. It is all
right. Water iris
is in bloom. We miss
nothing, whisper as tall

grasses whisper when a soft wind
spreads meaningless rumors. Wind
rises. It is too
dark to see the blue
iris, blue disciplined

to a cause. The overturned
canoe glimmers like unearned
praise in the moonlight,
floating pure pyrite,
just as bright. Unconcerned

as we seem now, later we'll lie
awake, listening as we try
to sleep the night through,
dreamless, listening to
the mockingbird sing lie
after beautiful lie.

Woods Water
Moving Picture Poem

The woods I pass are of a color no more.
They dapple their green with gold
as they float into their slow fall.

I've lived too long under water.
It's time for me to float in a slow fall
to the surface, counting on currents,
counting on slack water before flood tide,
counting on slack water before ebb tide.
At the ebb: counting on the slow fall
of the water.

Shore souvenirs, glass fisherman's floats
hang in the window, a freeze frame
to catch the slow fall of light.
The picture moves at sixteen frames a second
to stop my counting frames,
to stop my slow fall.

Night Visit

I woke to bones.
Feral gnawing, feral claws
scrabbling against metal.
Such a short leap from the cans
to the low shed just under my window.
How useless the screens
against such claws.

Each day at dusk the yard slipped away
to a wilderness I would not enter.
Yet tonight as bones cracked
and claws scratched while I listened,
I thought to walk out into the night.

But it was damp and the flashlight
would be weak against the moonless night.
I left my bed and crept across the hall
where in the spare room I lay
cradled in the too soft mattress,
straining to listen to the distant feast.

Birds

Even before the fog lifted,
crows stalked the lawn, imperious,
coughing at morning.
Now afternoon light falls
golden through the trees;
shadows stretch across the lawn.
The wind comes up from the sea.
The woods quiver with wind
and light at summer's end.
Terns blown inland, wheel and scree.
Mourning doves, wings whirring, fly off.
Deep in the woods an owl's question
brackets the day.
I have been too long away
from the sound of your voice.

Souvenirs

Nothing tacky, of course:
no clamshell jewelry, sand candles,
wooden gulls or coffee mugs.

But this brush holder
used by Chinese scholars
is finely carved with figures, flowers
and a poem (I am told)
neither of us could read.
Unaccountably I remember wisteria
still heavy with early morning rain.
You would place this empty ivory
in your unused sunken parlor
hung with blue brocade.
I'd rather you kept it in the clutter
of your room, stuffed with pens.

Or perhaps
you might like
this white jade
luminous
cool smooth fruit
would grow warm
in your hands.

The long way goes up Melody
winding down Pleasant
past gray cedar-shingled cottages
with careless gardens and singed lawns.
In one front yard a large gray rock
on raked orange earth.
All summer I wait for the planting
while on gray fences
a riot of wild roses buds, blooms, fades.
The rock remains shimmering in the heat, solid.

Farther on down by Deep Hole Road
guys toss a baseball around
trying nothing fancy,
the solid thud of the ball in mitts,
voices rise and fall.

At the bottom of Pleasant Street
on either side rise hills,
houses whose windows look out over water.
A stand of pines, widely spaced,
formal, neat, tamed,
marks one yard where young boys might play
mornings before skittering down the steep drive,
buckets and shovels in hand.
Behind shut windows the curtains are still

in the closed breathless house
empty between families.
I stop to watch,
thinking about familiar strangers
in their rented sunny kitchen,
their breakfasts, fruit, buttered toast,
eggs frying and bacon.

The short cut starts
on a washed-out road then takes
the first footpath into the woods
where in the shade grow tall grasses, vines,
a few spindly flowers.
Then a street, suburban, neat,
and suddenly a stretch of sandy road
cut through woods.
Here in high grass growing by the land
I stoop, trying to memorize flowers.

Uphill, underbrush thick, woods filled
with mysterious rustles and half-seen movements.
After a quick view of wetlands,
more civilization, then down
a steep terraced trail
bursting with beach plums.

•

At the bottom, I look up the hill
at the stand of pines, formal,
the house closed
between families.

Catechism

Just for a moment she may have paused,
adjusting her hair in the mirror:
negligent, that's the effect she wanted,
entering the room where her lover waited.

Might she have paused, too,
in the doorway, leaning against the jamb,
reciting her catechism: the question,
"Is there nothing more?"
and answered as she'd been taught,
"Make do."

Middle Age

Years ago we hung a bear's head in the upstairs hall,
for we had faced down death in a distant wilderness.

Now we fill in small landscapes with washes
as we settle for chatter. Memory is the bawd

of time; the past is tricked out. We wait for
time to dull memory. We forget their alliance;

we look to forgetfulness for solace,
forgetting the shadow on the stair, the real menace.

A u b a d e

Over his body, her horizon,
she watched the dawn alone.
And when a brief cascade of notes
left the room awash in sound,
he silenced Schubert with a touch.
He pulled the blanket up to shield
his face from light.
His body lay as in a winding sheet.
She knew one day she'd look into his face,
his eyes wide and blind, unwrap him
dead to the world.

Infestations

Stunning, how suddenly destruction
occurs: cereals ruined,
carpets consumed, floor supports
crumbled—the air of the closed house
a storm of wings.

Infestations begin with seeming innocence:
a single weevil, a flutter of soft gray wings,
a lone beetle, or its larva, a living comma.
How easy to turn away
magnanimous, let it be, or
crush it casually, not searching for more.
Unconscious cunning, insidious, in darkness,
until the infestation is complete.

S h a r d s

At dawn the shards of glass
embedded in the wall gleam
like slabs of river ice upended.

The shards assume enormous
proportions, dangerous
even from the safety
of the kitchen window where
I sit watching through the dawn.

A cat steps fastidiously
among the shards, remains
unharmed, gathers herself inward
for the leap to ground. Among
them she seems gargantuan;
in spite of the brick wall beyond
I cannot shift my vision
properly to see the shards small;
I recognize this as an error
in perspective, fixed.

Better to go about my business,
finding small purchases.
Shreds of dreams cling
like lint to my shawl.

I wrap myself for warmth,
gathering myself inward.

In late morning the shards glisten,
resemble bright ice broken;
they are nothing but broken bottles,
pieces upended; they are all things broken
and dangerous, a warning off, a warning
away. I tell myself, go; stay.

Ritual

I dust books, polish silver,
wash crystal, wax furniture,
wanting everything you take away
to be perfectly cared for,
wanting to be free
from reproaches.

The place is piled with things.
Cartons glut the rooms and spill
into the hall under the eyes
of neighbors.

Past midnight,
all our feeling squandered,
we sleep.

You can't get the keys out of the case,
and hand it to me to break
my nails, cursing our incompetence.
We both know
you'll never return
but I want to lock you out.
The movers haul away what's left.
Everything of value you
carried off long ago.

·

The men unroll mats on the floor
and lay out your suits and your coats.
These they cart unceremoniously
like inconvenient corpses
from a garden party.
I want to be wearing hat and gloves.
The rooms are stripped bare,
the closets emptied,
the drawers twice turned.
Nothing is left to muffle the echoes
in these high-ceilinged spaces.
Alone now, at last I can begin
to know my place.

Clairvoyant

An unwilling eavesdropper,
I hear your voice
across the room,
across the city.

Between us
many dwellings.
I hear your footsteps,
the clatter of dishes.

Memories spill
rattle scatter
like a string
of beads broken.

Your voice twines
around hers,
continuous,
knots into lace
of an old pattern.

The lace rises
to the skylight;
floats, a dark web;
hovers, a fine net
and strong.

Elegy for a Woman

My husband always bent
to kiss her first.
I watched her
lift her hand
to brush his face
with her fingers.
At the base of her nails
were small pink moons.

Her body was filled
with broken promises.

She held herself apart,
hating to be kept close,
but for a long time
she, her lover, my husband
and I were anchored
together.

I watched her
face grow pale.
Her hair fell forward,
obscuring her features.
Slowly she turned
away from me.

•

All my life
I have wanted to be
someone else.

Yardwork

"Two paradises 'twere in one
to live in Paradise alone."
— Marvell, "The Garden"

To the forsythia's golden abandon
he made an end. Leaning breathless,
swift-sheared, he pruned against the season.
The branches tumbled, a pyre at his feet.
She'd loved the wild forsythia,
had coaxed blooms,
had filled the house
with crystal vases of sunlight.
Now the bush took shape, tamed.

Back and forth he pushed the mower,
squaring the lawn: hated the fallen
magnolia petals pale as she was, ever
winter pale. He cut through hillocks
of violets. Each spring she'd begged
him not to mow, leaving ink bottles
and spice jars of violets here and there,
purple and unexpected as a bruise.
He marched, determined to annihilate
or at least evade these
memories of all she'd made.

The Copper Bowl

He'd invited her to luncheon on his terrace.
"In summer I like to dine *al fresco*," he said,
"and it would give me great pleasure
if you'd be my guest.
I'm no fine chef, but if you'll take your chances..."

"Dine," she thought, "I'll bet you dine.
Don't you ever eat?"
But she'd accepted
and now found herself sitting at the table
he'd so carefully set
with calculated imperfections
of mismatched plates and polished crystal
to say, "No woman
lives here."

On the table
a few sprigs of argeratum
and coleus paid modest tribute.
Coleus and argeratum edged the terrace
in neatly weeded beds;
at the corners pink geraniums
bloomed in whitewashed pots.
The greenest of lawns
sloped gently down from the terrace
where they sat at luncheon.

•

Omelette aux tomates.
She picked at the food and thought
of Henry James and
of the virtuous attachments she'd had.
They marched across her plate
in dress whites.

She looked at her host:
"Who is this man?" she was wondering
when she saw a gnat laboring
across the checkered linen.
The chilled wine in the glasses
all covered with beads of water
caught the sunlight.

She thought of picking
off the gnat;
she thought of putting
a cube of ice in its path
and changing its climate,
thought of the spreading stain
of cool water;
thought of plucking
a bean from her salad
and holding it redolent
with garlic and oil and vinegar
near the gnat
in an olfactory heaven.

Even, she thought
of discreetly crushing
the gnat
into the checkered cloth.
Entertaining these thoughts,
diverted,
she smiled.

He'd seen the gnat too,
thought it merely
another perfect imperfection
and dismissed it
from his thoughts.
He noticed her smile and was pleased;
turned his attention
to the copper bowl of fruits
and was pleased with the rich colors
of apricots and peaches and bananas
and grapes in the copper
of the bowl that had survived
the division.

And he turned away
from the bowl
and from the woman
at the table
and he looked out

over the greenest of lawns
that sloped down away from the terrace
away from the empty house
where he was at last master.

Portrait

"But that was in another country,
and besides, the wench is dead."
— Marlowe, *The Jew of Malta*

The man who murdered his wife
writes poems we read
looking for traces of blood
or regret, finding none.
The poet gentles us.
We listen for an echo
of her scream
as pushed backwards
over the balcony
she fell to silence.
We read the poems
sniffing for the first hint
of death: the body dismembered
in a trunk in the closet;
or the odor seeping
from the ground raked smooth
under the picnic table.

Other men simply starve their wives
to bloodless, blameless deaths.
The husks of these women
blow through the streets.

They hold themselves apart
from other wives, guarding
their shameful secret
until they are charged
with being aloof,
self-centered, empty.
No one suspects the husband
who grows greedily fat,
who writes no poems.

Seafood

The bag torn open yields
blind eyes, claws, a heap
of armored bodies and salt
air, smelling of tide pools.
I dump the red corpses,
and I smell summer.

Sticky with salt and thirsty,
we drank beer, cold and bitter.
We said, "Grasses, water,
ducks..." We said, "The whole
Maine seacoast..." We said,
"The pleasure of daytrippers..."

Night does not fall; it rises
from the marsh. Greens and blues
leach watercolors into the air.

Sometimes I think that if
you had kept me, I might
have died in silence.

Assemblage: Altered Object

Imagine those parts of me
you single out for praise
in a box partitioned
arranged by Cornell:

in one place
my hair neatly coiled

in another compartment
my teeth
a mysterious heap

to the side
my toes
straight and curling
pink

in the center
my hands
a pale lotus
unfolding.

•

Impossible.
I am uncontained,
untamed,
unperfectible
even
in the narrow coffin
of your praise.

A   Woman's   Poem

1. Metamorphosis

I gild my lids green
then blink at the image
in the mirror, stare
heavy-lidded, and suspicious
of reflections.
Again and again
run my sullen tongue
over cracked lips,
finding no pleasure
in mirrors or
pooled reflections.
A gilded amphibian,
I have surrendered
my rights to drowning,
have become a survivor
of receding landscapes
and changing climates.

2. Exile

Gilded, lizard-lidded,
newly cousined to the
crawling squamous-skinned,

to tortoises, toads and frogs,
I am no longer at home
in my husband's house
where rooms collapse
like drinking cups;
where an infant cries
for milk, and I, amphibian now,
have none to give suck.

3. Confiteor

In the lab
we fished our frogs
from buckets of formalin.
My frog, tilting,
seemed to leap
from the tray,
from the yellow wax
and the pinholes.
I found her filled
with flowers of eggs;
those I cut and scraped away
impatient to begin.

4. Return

Once in August
near weed-grown margins of water
I found a toad, still as a dream,
freckled brown as a sparrow,
dusty, sun-warmed, throbbing
in my palm, held
for a moment there.
Now, in the hollow of my throat,
my fingers like wings,
I feel in my palm a reckless pulse,
and I remember the toad
and the lake dimpled with sunlight
and I feel for a moment again
the fullness of summer.

Challenge

Frances Scheiber Kotzin 1905-1983

1. *solanum melongena*

I never saw an eggplant trellised,
yet a hundred years ago
aubergines
were grown along walls commonly
as roses would be now.
These tender ornamentals:
leaves oblate, lobed;
flowers violet, pendant
solitary pendant flowers finally
giving way to pendulous fruit,
prized shining aubergines.

Though she never saw an eggplant trellised,
still in her kitchen garden
my mother, shy, defiant,
grew aubergines for the beauty
of the flowers alone.

2. *solanum tuberosum*

All we see is scraggle:
stems, leaves, insignificant flowers
(insects, fungi, bacteria, virus, blight),
while underground on rhizomes
tubers slowly grow.

Once my mother lifted
from the red vegetable bin
a sprouting potato,
showed me how
to cut it for planting.

She sectioned off a far corner of the garden
and talked plainly about insects,
fungi, bacteria, virus, blight.
Squatting, she taught me
to prepare the earth properly.
"Plant these," she said. "Take care.
Wait. Have patience, faith."

Seder

"And the Holy One, blessed be He,
came and killed the Angel of Death."
— *Chad Gadya*

The host is eager to begin.
Like a too familiar uncle, the Angel
of Death circles the table.
The first question:
whose turn.

Alone, my mother
and I refuse the dining room
and sit side by side
in easy chairs. "Behold.
This is the bread of affliction."

We dip parsley in salt water, but when
I open the front door, only winter's
breath bears in
on the blue light.

Elijah's glass stands full.
I have said all the blessings. I
do not use
my father's cup.

•

I raise and lower the plate,
reading all the words. We complete
the service, but at the end we do not
choose to sing
Chad Gadya.

Checklist

I remember a waiting room
but not the color of the walls.

I remember a nurse
but not what she looked like.

I remember a gurney
but not how it got there.

I remember a sheet
but not who removed it.

I remember talking
but not what I said.

I remember smoothing her hair
but not when I kissed her.

I remember her blue and white dress
but not if she wore perfume.

I remember touching her hands
holding nothing.

Gravesite

The trowel of earth cold in my hand,
my father gone past finding,
my mother boxed, floating
in seepage, I look into a common grave.

My grave, too, kindly excavated
for a sneak preview,
a grave-diggers' whim;
administratively careless
to let me spy out my own place
close to the stone.
Left alone, I would choose
to sprawl sideways, occupying
both plots, like a lonely woman
making the best of an empty bed.

Reclaiming the Dead

My father stumbled into death.
We'd turned away a moment,
then a call.
The next spring my mother and I
planted violets that never grew back.
The cemetery has rules, no flowers,
we learned as we stooped
planting around his footstone anyway.

All winter the earth, unyielding,
refused everything.
Now the ground gives under-foot
as I cross the field,
wary as a trespasser.

My mother telephoned her death;
when she died I was on my way.
It rained through the night
after I bought her coffin.
It was ritually correct, the pine
box, pegged. New to my hands,
her rings cut my fingers
as I carried her there, daughter, pall-
bearer, talking to her steadily
since her death. The gravediggers let go.

I heard the splash. I saw her float.
A pump, a purposeful machinery,
worked until she was settled.

I make my way to the woods,
to the path down to the swollen cedar stream,
loops of brambles,
greening, have caught the hang
of spring.

Housekeeping

The women knew what they were doing.
Sometimes I think of them,
her friends, Rose and Grace,
efficient, bent over her bed, stripping it,
smoothing the fresh sheets, stooping
to make hospital corners tucked tight.
I must have been gone hours for all
the laundry to have been folded away. Even
then I wanted to sleep in the nest of her bed.

For a long time the house held
the smell of stale smoke like an echo
as though I wanted that, too, kept close.

Mother, forgive me. I have been
making changes. Nothing is just
as you left it. Some things are past
saving, gone through slow erosion.
Still, each spring I take down the worn
curtains to wash by hand. You grew
breathless, expanding the narrow task
to teach me, hoping your keeping house
would, for another round of seasons, last.

Keeping Time

Always before, you had been nimble.
While 78's whirled, your pink
satin-slippered feet traced
graceful patterns round and round
in perfect time. You held my hands
high above my head,
laughing partners. So you taught
me how to dance, to enter
a room with grace, to please
and thank, to welcome, to pen
the proper note.
                    Here, too,
it all counts; the slow IV,
a calibrated beaker, screens monitor
what one calls your progress.
Not all these tubes and wires together
can keep you tethered. I feed you ice
chips like pomegranate seeds.

Mother, I promise to remember
your beauty. I study your face,
seek your errant pulse, learn
from you one more, this last, the
necessary lesson.

Harvest

All the sweet green apples
have fallen to ground.
They lie like eggs in nests,
in grass grown long, bent and matted.
These apples are not meant
for the cider press.
Who owns this orchard now,
no matter; a windfall
for strangers, the apples
belong to whoever takes the care
to gather them.

I bend at the waist;
my back warms in the sun,
but my bones know autumn.
If I should wake
early on the right day
not long from now
I'd see from my window
the world hazed
with the shimmer
of first frost.

Today the grass is wet with dew.
My feet, my legs, are drenched
as I move among the trees.
I snare my foot in a creeper,
stumble, but catch myself,
and bend again to gather
the small green apples.
The basket's slow to fill.
No rush this morning to harvest.

This year autumn is more to me
than a light as yellow as chrysanthemums,
than a windfall of sweet green apples
in an abandoned orchard.
I feel the season:
frost soon, winter certain.

Lois Lane Courts Death

Remember how it went on TV.
Kryptonite didn't kill
George Reeves.

In this strip, from panel to panel
the details accrue. Tonalities
are lost in the printing.

Lois primps. Only she does not
recognize the profile of her lover
in his disguise. He seems
so mild-mannered. The space
of their silence separates them.

An unexplained shadow fills
the foreground of the panel.

She knows that her lover can be had
in a speeding bullet,
in a leap from a tall building.
She rejects this as clumsy technology,
as melodrama.

·

She decides instead to let him
make the significant advances,
decides instead to wait for death
who comes to her slowly courting
breath, by breath, by breath.

Still Life

Twinned, torn, you laughed out
of tune. You locked yourself
away for a full month.

The bell is broken, its cap missing, but
on faith I ring, am answered. Doors
are unlocked, slammed shut. I approach you through
corridors, guided, guarded, passing through smoky
wards, inquire of the matron have you had a good day.

Near your room is a still
life, a row of beige pottery neatly
arranged on a shelf, orderly, tame,
in place, patently empty.

You want pepperoni pizza; I translate,
"I want to go home." Instead I smooth
your hands with lotion; stroke your hair.

After a week, they take you off watch.
With limited privileges, you
venture beyond one locked door
into the cramped courtyard.

In a damp November the summer
furniture, white wrought iron, remains,
a sad joke. I look for swings, think
of chains twisting, realize how
the courtyard is swept clean of danger.

The starry night still swirls through bare branches.
Gradually this becomes a familiar world,
the news of the day: fresh salad,
the pay phone is across from your room,
a rapist is newly admitted to your ward,
the door to your room doesn't lock,
a loony letter to the mayor is answered,
you learn that all the self-destructive women
here have a history of abuse, you begin to care
about the others, they put you back on watch.

We offer one another what we can. We
call each other by name. We braid
and unbraid hair and fingers. We talk
about husbands and lovers, speak in soft
sentences that begin, "When I was a wife..."
Carefully we unravel old lies.
I roll the words "normal lives" in my
mouth like marbles. I try to speak around them.

•

We look into one another like mirrors
that stretch, swell, attenuate.
We stoop, stand on tiptoe, finally eye to eye,
gain managed grace, measured reason.

You forbear. You regain
privileges. You learn to live with loss.

D a n c e r s

"That is no country for old men."
— Yeats

Nor this for women
who growing old
as the slow spiral of years unwinds
move as though descending
unfamiliar stairs
or sit in stolen leisure
on garden chairs
talking of husbands and lovers
and of the inadvisability of affairs,
testing trust and wisdom.
We do not outgrow
our vaulted chambers.

Jane swims at the university pool
where young women are untouched
by gravity,
their legs unmarked by veins
as though their beautiful bodies
were bloodless.
Shulamith in Jerusalem
attends the Turkish baths.

From tiled rooms women rise to sun
themselves, hair streaming
in golden light.
We three sit under locust trees,
stir black coffee
with cinnamon bark,
nibble the sweet spicy sticks,
never once mentioning
Michelangelo.

Phaedra paces, desire's fool.
She is blinded by a double vision,
sees the best of absent Theseus
in his son, whose muscles are so perfectly
articulated that her blood beats
to the pulse of Hippolytus.
To him she is invisible even as she burns.
It is the tragedy of her age.

We reluctantly rise
bearing our cups back
to the kitchen,
having settled nothing
and glad of it.

Mystery Lovers

The world is filled with perfect crimes.
Strangers are guilty; neighbors, more so.
Mystery lovers imagine unspeakable passions
and shameful ancestries. They whisper conspiracy.

Such habits of perception endure.
If not justice, then niggling wrongs
are obsessions. Actions are turned
like rocks to watch the motives squirm.

Only in books are ambiguities resolved.
Characters align themselves with evil
or good. Wickedness is vanquished,
granting exigencies of plot. Who
are these mystery lovers seen only
from a distance, then obliquely,
who never speak of themselves?

Lycanthropy

Especially for a woman the change
is painful, to watch my nails grow thick,
the hair on my body lengthen and coarsen.
Difficult, too, to be the subject of speculation.
I, who had always seemed so
conventional, suddenly afflicted.
I suffer the whispers of neighbors,
rightfully suspicious of my knowledge
of darkness, of unexplained bloodstains.

Unpleasant to be forced to wander,
night after night from village to village.
To be sure, there is more to it than hiding
in ditches, slinking up to the lonely cottage,
hunted by men made brutal by fear.
I am not expecting your sympathy.
I am afraid there is something messy,
unladylike about my acquired appetite,
about giving in to compulsion.
But something attractive, too.
Power, locks falling away, doors flying open.
Knowing I am the calm center of terror.

•

Myself childless, I began by devouring
my sisters' children, as is the custom.
It could have been a dead giveaway
when I did not join the women wailing
at the funeral. The remains
surrounded by watchers were no more
to me than my leavings.

Understand. Others have had a taste
for young flesh, have sinned and escaped
loathsome transformations. True,
it is a misfortune to be singled out,
to be made into a moral lesson,
tiresome to become an example.
But I have never had patience
with women given to self-pity.

ABOUT THE AUTHOR

Miriam N. Kotzin, associate professor of English at Drexel University, directs the Certificate Program in Writing and Publishing and teaches creative writing and literature. Her fiction and poetry have been published widely in literary journals. She is a contributing editor of *Boulevard* and a founding editor of *Per Contra: The International Journal of the Arts, Literature and Ideas*. She is the author of *A History of Drexel University* (Drexel University, 1983) and two collections of poetry, *Reclaiming the Dead* (New American Press, 2008) and *Weights & Measures* (Star Cloud Press, 2009).

www.ingramcontent.com/pod-product-compliance
Lightning Source LLC
LaVergne TN
LVHW091156080426
835509LV00006B/715